Overcoming OCD and Schizophrenia with God in My Life

Overcoming OCD and Schizophrenia with God in My Life

Chip Correll

Writers Club Press

San Jose New York Lincoln Shanghai

Overcoming OCD and Schizophrenia with God in My Life

Writers Club Press
an imprint of iUniverse.com, Inc.

For information address:
iUniverse.com, Inc.
620 North 48th Street, Suite 201
Lincoln, NE 68504-3467
www.iuniverse.com

ISBN: 0-595-12147-0

Printed in the United States of America

ACKNOWLEDGMENTS

This book would not have been made possible if not for the constant nurturing love of my family and friends. Many of these beloved people took time out of their busy schedules to proofread and edit the text in my book.

They say that it takes a tribe to raise a child to adulthood, and I find this to be very true in my case.

I'd like to thank all my teachers who taught me how to think and ensured that I will be a contributor to the betterment of our world.

I especially want to thank my mom, dad, Dennis, John and my extended family and friends for their support and encouragement to this project.

Most of all, I thank God for using me as His vessel to hopefully better the lives of those touched by this book. Thank you, and read on!

DEDICATION

I dedicate this book to my family. My mom, dad, Dennis, brother and entire family have really been there for me through my bouts with mental illnesses. Their constant support is greatly appreciated. I pray that God blesses all of my family as He has blessed me with them.

Contents

Foreword

by
John Correll

Mental illness affects millions of people in all walks of life without regard to age, race, sex, marital status or socioeconomic and educational background. It rears its head in mysterious ways, sometimes without warning. It can appear at any stage of a person's life and when it does, acceptance can be the hardest part. Though it may appear to be an individual disease, mental illness affects the entire family. Denial, misunderstanding and confusion are the usual reactions for the so-called "sane" family members. Understanding and awareness are vital if we are to be able to offer support to those suffering with such diseases. This book is presented to offer insight into one man's story about how mental illness has touched him.

As brother to the author, I've known Chip Correll since the day he was born. I've witnessed his growth from younger brother, whom I could overpower and control as a child, to a man who has surpassed me in stature. Not unlike other children, he was a boy of energy, ambition, fears and dreams. Outside the unique qualities that make us all individuals, there were no signs that he was different in any way. His passion for music fueled his desire to make contacts within the music and entertainment industry. He appeared to be afraid of nothing and headed for success. As a bright student, the world lay before him for his conquest.

One day many years later, I received a call that Chip was institution-alized. He had gone into some sort of "trance" and was voluntarily checked into a mental facility. I'm not sure of anything more shocking than the news that day. It was an event that seemed implausible, surely nothing like that could happen in my family. It was my own ignorance of mental illness that made it seem shameful and unimaginable. Since that time I have only begun to understand the dynamics of mental illness and how common Chip's story is.

Though I've always known Chip to be a religious person, the depths of spiritual guidance in the author's life become apparent throughout the content of this book. He derives much of his strength and direction through his personal conversations with God. It is this strength that has allowed him to adapt and overcome his struggle with mental illness. Chip is a generous person who volunteers his time serving his community through the local news media and has achieved success on many levels.

It is always a tragedy when bad things happen. Arguably, no one would consider mental illness to be a blessing. However, we all gain insight when one strips down the barriers of fear and stigma and allows their story to be heard for the benefit of understanding. About to unfold before you is the story of one man's struggle with mental illness. It is an eye-opening account of the courage it takes to live with mental illness on a daily basis. Perhaps it could be said that the ultimate act of generosity is sharing one's inner self. You the reader are about to receive the gift of insight. This is Chip's story. Enjoy!

John Correll

1

Introduction/God in my Life

I laid on the couch, my blurred eyesight staring at the white ceiling above me, fans swirling overhead. I felt tired, dismayed and disoriented. "Where am I?" I asked myself weakly.

As I awoke, sun was shining through the windows from the East. All I remembered from that morning was that the night before my parents and the police took me to a local public mental health facility.

"Time to get up!" yelled one of the medical technicians working on the morning shift. "Time for meds and breakfast."

Looking around, I saw that there were about five doors on each side of the large room I had slept in on a couch the night before, with open doors showing that there were three to four persons in each room.

Then it came back to me, the events leading to what had put me here.

I had arrived at the hospital just after midnight because I thought my grandma Ruth—who, in reality, loves me very much—was going to kill me.

"No! You're going to kill me!" I pleaded with the nurse, extending his palm with a pill on it.

"Here, this will relax you," said the nurse, extending his palm with a pill on it.

"No, I won't take it!" I said, panicking. There were three or four other technicians guarding the door I had just walked through. They separated me from the security of my mom and step-dad, Dennis.

I was terrified by then, because the nurse threatened to give me a shot unless I swallowed the feared pill. I reluctantly agreed to take the medicine they offered me. Then I settled back and let the pill do its work. I relaxed and fell asleep in the lobby. I later learned the medicine I took was used to combat psychosis—or the loss of touch of reality—which is what I was experiencing when I felt people wanted to kill me that night.

One Scripture in particular stands out in my mind as helping me get through my stay in the mental hospital. It is: "Do not let your hearts be troubled. Trust in God; trust also in me." John 14:1 Reciting this Scripture, I felt comfort in the Lord, just knowing that He is always there for me.

March, 1995, was a turn-around month for me. First of all, I was put on medications I had never even heard of before. I was told that I'd have to take medications for schizophrenia for the rest of my life. Oh great! Just what a 23-year-old male needs to hear!

After I left the hospital, my psychiatrist diagnosed me with having obsessive-compulsive disorder (OCD) and schizophrenia.

When you're in your teens and early 20's you tend to think that nothing can stop you—or slow you down—from achieving whatever you want, and that the future is bright and full of promises. Family, new cars and a beautiful new house seemed to be birth-rights of every American. Boy, was I wrong!

Today I live on a fixed income. I receive Social Security Disability. My doctor's appointments are covered through Medicare and my medications are covered by my state's Medicaid program.

My feelings towards the Lord may be found in Psalms 136: "Give thanks to the Lord, for He is good. His love endures forever."

Schizophrenia altered all that I had previously known to be rational, making my world one full of uncertainties. It's a miracle that I've made it this far, and I attribute my faith in God for my ability to pull myself through the rough spots.

I wasn't always a "Jesus Freak." That's what some church no-goers call the people who attend my non-denominational church, at which the Holy Bible is the core. I feel that it's unfair for people to label me a "Jesus Freak." How people can be so unaware of the mighty power of God working in all our lives astounds me.

In junior high school I was first introduced to the concept that one must accept Jesus into his heart in order to go to heaven. My grandma Ruth took me to her church, the Assembly of God, which is similar to inter-denominational churches. I found the kids in my Sunday school class friendly and kind, but all the hands-raising and chanting in church really made me feel uncomfortable.

Psalms 134 says: "Praise the Lord, all the servants of the Lord who ministers by night in the house of the Lord. Lift up your hands in the sanctuary, and bless the Lord."

My parents divorced when I was 10 years old which shattered my spirit. Now I feel God was preparing me for greater things in my life, and getting saved was His number one priority in my life. Reaching out to other Christians and non-believers, I trust, is God's close second goal for my life.

I believe God speaks to each of us through the people we encounter and talk with. The circumstances, trials and tribulations He puts us through are tests to prepare us for living the life we are called to by God.

So I was seeking something greater than I had found here on Earth. My Mom is super, but even she lets me down sometimes.

When I was 12 years old I was on my knees—literally—when I invited the Lord into my heart. Mom and grandma Ruth prayed separately and together that my brother and I be saved.

I was in the sixth grade when I was saved. The divorce was emotionally hard on dad. Becoming a born-again Christian helped him heal. My dad became born-again a few years after the divorce, which was very hard on him emotionally and spiritually.

Some people talk about radical changes in their lives when they are "saved." I didn't experience a radical change right away, but maybe that's because I was so young. Salvation is a one-time thing.

When I was baptized—totally submerged in 1996 in water before my church congregation—I gave all my problems to the Lord in total submission. What an uplifting experience!

Today, I live my life by asking God every morning to use each and every one of His children as vessels for His work; in other words, make us His servants.

I believe with all my heart that God's love does conquer all. It's a fact in my life, God's love affects everything I do.

I was raised to believe Joshua 24:15: " Choose for yourselves this day whom you will serve. As for me and my house we will serve the Lord."

I was born in 1971, to John and Deloris Correll, my birth parents, who named me Charles after my grandfather, but I got my nickname by chance.

Before I was born my parents were driving in a rural area and came across a house. Out front was a sign with all of the family members' names on it. At the bottom was the name "Chip." My parents decided that if they were to have another son, their second, that they would nickname him Chip.

My nickname has stuck with me ever since. God and my nickname have carried me through many hard times. I say my nickname has carried me through many hard times because of what Chip stands for.

Chip means "little" or "insignificant" in dictionary terms. I believe that things aren't always as they appear, and my nickname is no exception.

My faith in God is as great as the highest mountain. As my story unfolds, a pattern becomes clear. A pattern that indicates that God has been with me every step of the way, through it all.

As believers in Christ, the Holy Spirit lives in each of us. This is good to know. The Holy Spirit speaks to us in what others say to us, what we speak and the events that God puts in our way. Remember: the Holy Spirit is one-third of the Trinity. God and the Lord make up the other two parts of the Trinity.

Through my mental illness and my bouts with schizophrenia, God has uplifted and enlightened me. He walks with me every day, all the time. Just like in the "Footprints" scene and poem, in which God carries His child through his or her troubles and therefore there is only one set of footprints in the sand. I love this picture! I relate to the child in this poem.

God is an active part of my life. Not only do I read the Holy Bible almost daily and attend church, Bible Studies, Prayer Meetings and Pre-marital classes, I also make Christian music an integral part of my everyday life.

Where would the beastly man be without music which soothes and inspires the savage beast within each of us.

Music plays a great part in my life. From my early days idolizing rock stars to more recent days listening to Christian hymns and rock or pop melodies, music is the mainstream, the lifeblood of my life.

Music has always been a great inspiration to me. I love music as much as I love life. I believe that life and music are intertwined. What would a world without music be? Music entertains me. Songs help people to express their inner feelings. For me, music is an outlet for my frustrations, disillusionment and inspiration.

Music kept the slaves sane and full of hope for a better life. Their hearts sang out melodies praising their Lord regardless of their lots in life. Music helped slaves cope because it allows them—by escaping into music—to take their pain and turn it into inspiration.

Pain inspires music. Music soothes one's pain and allows for a healthy release of emotions. Music is meant to lift up God. Psalm 150 reads: "Praise the Lord. Praise God in His sanctuary; praise Him in His mighty heavens. Praise Him for His acts of power; praise Him for his surpassing greatness. Praise Him with the sounding of the trumpet, praise Him with the harp and lyre, praise Him with tambourine and dancing, praise Him with the strings and flute, praise Him with the clash of cymbals, praise Him with resounding cymbals. Let everything that has breath praise the Lord. Praise the Lord."

This is the story of my life. This book is intended to inspire and enlighten the reader. This is what I desire to do, to be God's messenger and miracle worker. I desire to enrich the lives of those I touch, including those whom I my touch through this book or any of my other writings.

It is my prayer that you, the reader, will grow from reading my book. And may God always be in your heart, as He is with me. He is with each person already.

2

Dreamer

I am a dreamer. By nature, I have always been a dreamer.

Even with my faith in God, I've always idealized what could be rather than settling for what is. I've always like to stretch myself spiritually, academically and socially, knowing that God has always been there for me to catch me when I fall.

I'm a person who looks at the ideal and tries to figure out how we, as a nation and as a common people, can come together to achieve this ideal that I envision.

I feel life is so full of pain because it is when we are in pain that we grow the most. I don't believe in creating pain; there's enough of that in our world anyway. God is always with us, especially when we need Him the most in our lives.

I just wonder how things can be and why they aren't as they could be. Why are people hurting in today's society? I believe that without a strong anchor in God's Word and attending a home church, it becomes increasingly difficult to turn from temptations and live a God-inspired and God-centered life.

I believe that God made me a dreamer for a reason. I believe that God wants us to have more dreamers in this world of ours. Dreamers have always been great leaders in our world. Look at Abraham Lincoln and George Washington.

Since I've been a small child, I have dreamt that we would some day be able to erase color boundaries. I believe that God wants us all to accept the fact that we all are created equal. God has a plan for each of our lives, and our lives are intertwined just because God made us so.

Who is to say that being white is superior to someone who is black, and where does the difference come into play? Ignorance promotes prejudice; no one is any better than another person. Understanding and racial harmony promote love. Prejudice brings about hate.

I don't believe in "seeing" persons only by the color of their skin. Neither do I think or see in color. I believe that God created us all different, but equal.

Different, I believe, is the key word here. I don't believe that being equal is even an issue. Yes, we are all equal in birth, as a part of the human race. God created each of us equal and just as we are.

Why did God create each of us different, though? That's a good question that needs to be pondered here awhile.

We each are different, I believe, because God wants each of us to make a different contribution.

How can two identical people, if there were such a thing, make significantly different contributions? That's not possible, and so to get the most out of each of us, God created each of us different.

I am a dreamer who believes that God created different races and classes of people so that we each may be a contributing force in our world, and some day come harmoniously together in peace.

For each of us to become loving, we each are created different; in other words, what I am proposing is that God created each of us different so that we each may make a contribution and then learn to become more loving in the process.

I dream that one day men and women will truly walk together, hand in hand. For instance, why should men be paid more money for doing the same job as women? I believe it's unethical and unfair for men to make more than women for performing the same job. Things are getting better and better for women—and all of us as a society—every day as women and men grow closer in the wages.

The Holy Bible says that women are to submit to their husbands and that the men in turn are to treat their wives as their best friend. To me, this makes sense, but I think God intended to create a mutual bond when He included this in the Holy Bible.

I dream that one day we all will recognize and appreciate the wisdom and love that lives in many older people in our society. Why should older people lose respect in their old age in our society when they have so much to offer? Senior citizens are invaluable to the focus of the family staying together; grandparents help raise their grandchildren while an increasing number of husbands and wives are entering the workforce. Senior citizens also carry valuable real-life history lessons to share.

It is time, I, as a dreamer believe that we should look upon each man as a separate but integral part of our world.

Like a blade of grass in a meadow, we each make up an important part of the whole.

I believe in unity, for if we don't stand together then we all fall. We must all be together otherwise we all as a whole suffer.

Christ's words further identify the need for unity of all His children in Ephesians 4:2: "Be completely humble and gentle; be patient, bearing with one another in love."

I dream that one day there will be enough food, clothing, love and housing so that everyone can enjoy life to its fullest.

I believe that most of us are so concerned with "making it"—with paying our rent and buying groceries and wearing the finest clothes— that we actually forget that our neighbor, brother or sister is sick, hungry or dying. How can we let one person suffer while others live in excess? We must pray the "me-me" times will change to more charitable ones.

That's not to say that we each should feel guilty about succeeding financially.

My point is that life is beautiful and we each make up a beautiful blade of grass that makes us all whole and in order to truly thrive and live a life that is successful, we each must contribute whatever we can to the benefit of the whole.

Nothing matters more than each of us. This is what I'm trying to convey. If we all value each other equally to the next person, none of us would suffer.

There would be no poverty, no abuse, no alcoholism, no drug abuse, if we would just value one another for who and what we are.

Once we all truly gain this insight, through our faith, love and trust in God, then we each will hold the key to unlock our lives from the turmoil and bondage that we all live in. May God bless each of my readers with this insight.

3

Holy Spirit

God is a great inspiration to me. Without God, I wouldn't be here.

When I was down on my knees, truly on my knees and submitting to God, that's when I saw the light and was walking the closest to God.

I was in a mental institution in the Spring of 1995. I was admitted for being suicidal.

I was soon thereafter diagnosed as having atypical paranoid schizophrenia. I was put on trilafon to calm me down and to stop the psychotic thoughts. I thought that people in the mental institution I was in were trying to kill me. I had never been so scared in my entire life.

Never before, and never since, have I been hospitalized in a mental institution. I was terrified by this experience. Being in a mental institution is not much fun. First of all, you're under constant supervision and aren't free to take walks, smoke a cigarette (I don't smoke) or take showers whenever you want. The same thing holds true for eating. You are told when you can eat, much like any other hospital.

Nobody likes to feel ill. Mental Institutions help people who are ill. Simple logic points to the fact that people innately want to be well and not in places for the ill.

Finally, I was released from the local mental health hospital after four days. I don't know for sure today whether or not my life was in danger while in the mental institution.

I do know that up until this point in my life, I had always listened to how I felt to make decisions in my life.

I kept getting these gut feelings in the hospital, feelings that I should get up, for example, during breakfast and leave the room or get shot by one of the technicians. I was terrified, but I also was praying to God and reading the Holy Bible, and I feel that I have never walked so close to God as I did while on my knees in the hospital!

I believe that God got me through being in that mental institution. I prayed and read the Holy Bible to calm me down while I was there. There was nothing I could do to get out any faster, but my faith sustained me as I hit rock bottom there.

In the hospital I found solace in Isaiah 41:13: "For I am the Lord, your God who takes hold of your right hand and says to you, 'Do not fear; I will help you.'"

Prior to going to the hospital, I interned with a local talk show. I believe that God brought me to this point in my life as well.

I started the day by going to our local community college's Career Center, where I met with my long-time friend, Carrie, who is the Center's receptionist.

Carrie encouraged me to go back to a TV station where I applied. It was early afternoon when I walked into a local television station's lobby. A show was to be taped five minutes later that day. I had never watched the program, although I had heard of its host. I didn't even know what time the show was taped or what the topic for that day was.

Up until now, I was going to go back to school to become a school teacher. That day I was supposed to be in an orientation session for aspiring teachers.

But I felt "called" to work in communications. I told mom and Dennis this and they agreed with me that I should pursue this field. Because of this, I decided not to go to the orientation at the local university, from which I graduated in 1993 with a Bachelor's degree in English.

I have faith that when we pray and get into the Holy Bible—as I had done on my way over to the local television station's studios—God will lead us in His path.

A receptionist told me that interviews for the producer job, which I felt I really wasn't qualified for, would begin in a week or two.

I then asked what time the local show was being taped. She told me that the show would begin taping in five minutes, and asked me if I would like a ticket to the show.

I accepted and a security guard led me down a hall towards the studio. After the show, I introduced myself to the show's host. She asked me if I had applied for the producer job. I said "yes," and then after thinking for a moment she offered me an internship with the show! Just like that!

I "know" God brought me to this local talk show's studio. I never felt more at home and productive than when I interned with this top-rated program. God is always with us, but I felt especially close to the Lord during that Spring semester.

God does work miracles in the lives of His children; He lives in each of us. And since we are all His children, God works miracles in all of our lives.

God was with me and placed me in the right place at the right time when I entered that local television station. God gave me new challenges to overcome.

Every day of my internship I asked the Lord that everything I did would come from Him and glorify His name. Just pray and you'll see good things start happening to you.

It's important to recognize God's miracles when they happen. So often people neglect to realize that God is working in their lives and blessing them.

God means many things to me. Above all, God is faithful and provides for His children. He is always near.

I deeply believe in the Holy Trinity, in Jesus, God and the Holy Spirit.

I've seen the Holy Spirit at work in my life and in the lives I've encountered, far too often to ignore it. The Holy Spirit speaks all the time through people such as passing strangers, preaching pastors or caring teachers. When words honor God and seem to flow from your mouth, there's a good chance that it's the Holy Spirit at work. The true miracle, however, is in recognizing that God is a miracle and He's actively working in all our lives.

If it weren't for God, I don't think I would have made it through high school, the mental institution and through my challenging-and-yet-fun internship at a local television station.

God walks with each of us, even if we don't ask him to. But the truly beautiful work comes from the Higher Power I call God when we invite Him or Her into our lives.

We as believers in Christ need to gladly worship our Lord. Psalms 145:3 says: "Great is the Lord, and greatly to be praised."

4

Childhood

My earliest memories center around church. I remember being four years old and standing outside the church next to a bush getting my picture taken for Sunday school class. I remember my mom, dad and brother there. Those were happy times.

Mom has always been very encouraging and loving towards me and my brother, John.

I had fun in grade school. I remember doing coloring exercises in kindergarten and learning to write in cursive in the third grade. Being left-handed, my teacher kept a close eye on my writing style.

I had the same teacher in third and fifth grades. I remember directing and acting in plays before our classes back then.

I also gave oral reports for extra credit in science class (math and science don't agree with me very much at all; I'm a writer and love the English language!).

One report in particular sticks in my mind as a very painful experience. A fellow classmate and I were to give an extra-credit speech. It came to the night before our speech was due, and neither of us had done anything to prepare ourselves, no research or anything.

That night I scrambled to get some sort of speech ready. Since it was I who talked my friend into doing this speech, I took it upon myself to write the entire speech—both her part and mine—that night.

I opened an encyclopedia and looked up whatever our topic was (I forget what it was). To this very day I recall the public scolding our teacher gave us that day, as there were words in our speech that neither of us could even pronounce!

To this very day I, like millions of Americans, fear one of the greatest fears of man—public speaking! In part, I thank that teacher. I have found that with mild tranquilizers I can perform speeches with great ease.

Since I have anxiety as well as my other mental illnesses, my therapist told me that my speech phobia was due to a chemical imbalance quickly cured by taking half a mg of Clonazepam.

During my sixth grade, I was in "How the West was Really Won," a play about life on the Western frontier.

I played the part of the grandson. I remember a 45 second monologue that I had. I remember pacing our kitchen floor at home and timing my speech down to the very second on our microwave oven's clock!

I did great in the play!

Getting started with public speaking, for me, is always the hardest part. I now actually love public speaking once I get my feet wet!

All at one time my life changed overnight. All of a sudden Dad wasn't around anymore; it was like he had died.

I looked forward to my dad's visitations. I saw my dad once a week faithfully for about eight years. My dad, brother and I would go to the local mall, to the movies and to my favorite restaurants!

Today, we have a rather close and meaningful relationship.

I started seeing a grade school counselor when I was in the fifth grade, the year my parents got a divorce.

My counselor and I talked about my feelings a great deal of the time. Back then, my biggest problem was expressing my anger about my parents' divorce.

One day in the midst of our counseling session, my counselor had me act angry towards a male authority figure, the school's psychologist.

He and I both held long red pillows shaped in the form of big hot dogs. We battled back and forth, me hitting him and he hitting me back. I released a great deal of anger—constructively—in that session.

I remember being in the sixth grade and doing something really radical. For an honor roll student who never had even gotten into a fight, this was something radical for me—and most people. I married two classmates on the playground! I served as the marriage counselor and therefore brought the two of them together. The three of us were sent to the gymnasium, where we were separated and individually reprimanded.

To my thinking back then, marrying those two in a mock ceremony was fine because the two of them felt love for each other. I didn't know what true love and commitment were back then.

The principal readily excused me; this was atypical behavior—and never again repeated—for me. The other two kids were in special education classes for emotionally disturbed students; their teacher took care of handling the situation with them.

Kids in grade school were often brutal towards me, calling me names such as "gay," "queer" and "weird."

I recall the first day of gym class during my fifth grade. For me, that was the year that puberty and all those unanswered questions popped up. We also did taking showers after gym class.

I was the only one who protested to our gym teacher about having to take public showers. I felt ashamed of my slender body. I refused to take a shower with the rest of my school mates.

Back then, I thought bathing or taking a shower in public with other guys was gay; my peers thought I was gay because I didn't want to partake.

This is the turning point when my fellow classmates began calling me gay. This name-calling would taunt me all through high school.

5

High School

For me, high school was a time of inspiration. My true friends and family inspired me to think and dream big.

My best friend and "sister" in high school was a girl named Judy. She and I became friends during our freshman year of high school.

Our friendship grew over time. I believe that God works slowly sometimes in people's lives, and He did work slowly in this area and other areas of my life. My friendship with Judy grew steadily and slowly.

Judy and I took Spanish and General Psychology together and we competed for high grades. In doing so, Judy and I inspired one another to be and do our very best.

Active during high school in her church, Judy invited me to join her high school Sunday school. In addition to attending church and our high school group, we decided to join the choir.

Melissa, Betty, Frank, George and Kelley are some of my friends from high school who inspired me to achieve my goals and dreams.

So many of my classmates haunted me with their verbal insults that I learned to turn this criticism to my benefit. Rather than accept and take to heart their tongue-lashing, I turned lemons into lemonade and in doing so developed a very strong, healthy will to achieve great things, including my lofty goals.

I believe that success requires, among other things, lots of hard work. Yes, being in the right place at the right time and having ''connections'' do help, but in the end it takes hard work.

My high school years served me as a time of inspiration. We each go through different seasons in our lives, and for me the time of inspiration came when I was in high school.

I was really put down a lot in high school by my peers. I don't get ridiculed anymore, unless I do something really corny or stupid.

The more that people put me down, the more I became driven to succeed at high grades, work and even relationships.

I believe that the mind is an incredibly powerful tool, and if you want something bad enough, and pray, it will happen.

Like I said before, high school was a time of inspiration for me. I feel that when people constantly put you down, you either become an emotional cripple or you become stronger. Sometimes both can occur because love and constant abuse can be mixed together. Love heals while abuse destroys.

I think that my high school experiences made me a stronger person because I've learned to turn my back on trouble. I don't have the time nor energy for trouble.

High school is a confusing time for many students. Kids in high school just want to fit in. Being accepted is the ''cool'' thing in high school.

Lord only knows why I endured so much pain and ridicule in my high school years. Most everything that happens to us, if we allow God to enter our lives, inspires and prepares us for even greater feats and accomplishments.

Love—God's love—sees us all through our hard times. "Hard times knock, love will rock!" That's my motto in life. If times are hard, then pull closer to your support system and put your nose in the Holy Bible.

Friends, family and my faith in God got me through the high school torment, and the good times, also. Love saw me through it all!

I'll be honest with you. This is a difficult chapter to put into words, and may be hard for my sympathetic readers also.

High school was really a painful time for me. I'll cut right to the chase and be honest about it. For the most part, high school wasn't a fun time for me. At least not during school hours!

I recall one day taking a shower after gym class. Jim, also a junior at the time, pissed all over my legs for no apparent reason. I'm not sure to this day what Jim's problem was. I know I felt degraded by him, and rather than attacking him back, I held my anger in and later got rid of it by going for a long run later that night.

Every day on the school bus to and from the high school I attended there were spit-balls being shot at me. It was a disgusting experience, one in which I felt out-numbered and helpless. I've never again felt the same misery and demeaning hatred, thank God.

"Knock it off!" they mimicked me, like a sissy.

To this day, I cannot account for why some of my peers ridiculed me so. Either they thought I was gay and they hated gays or maybe they were jealous or attracted to me.

I was always the straight-arrow, honor-roll student that teachers took a liking to.

Only recently have I told my mom about my peers' making fun of me because I was too embarrassed at how I was being mistreated by my peers. Worse yet, I thought that what they told me—that I was gay—just might be true, and so I blamed myself for their rudeness. I remember hating, every morning and afternoon, getting onto that school bus; I dreaded the abuse. Occasionally a mature senior would stick up for me when I was a freshman or a sophomore.

My peers had nothing better to do but call me gay. I had even dated various girls in earnest during my high school years. My favorite girlfriend was Jennifer; she and I went to Homecoming our Senior year in 1988 and the Junior Prom in 1987. We had a great time!

Jennifer was conscious of her weight, but she was a healthy, sturdy girl, not scrawny and thin. Whenever we'd go out to dinner she'd only nibble at her food; she didn't like people watching her eat in public because she was so self-conscious.

Now that I think back, it's odd that she thought so poorly of her weight when it didn't matter at all to me.

Granted, I had terrific high school teachers who stood right beside me and taught me to the very best of their capabilities. My Spanish teacher was very tough, and to prove it I earned 14 credits at the college level for my foreign language proficiency!

Our student newspaper instructor was like a mother away from home to me. We still write one another and keep in touch that way.

Life gets so busy that we often forget the people who helped us get to where we're standing today. Life is complicated and often a mess, but the people who stand beside us are truly the only support, next to God, that we each have in this lifetime.

My mom is someone who loves me dearly and someone whom I care for deeply. My mother is a survivor who's been through some challenges in her life and has come back to tell her story about it. God bless her life, every day she has left!

My mom brought me up when I was down. Mom has always been a source of inspiration and encouragement to me. No matter what I wanted to do—as long as I'm not hurting myself or others—mom has always supported my decisions.

My mom is a very special lady. Mom and dad married in 1968. My brother John was born that first year. I was born two and a half years later. As about half of all married couples today, mom and dad eventually divorced.

John was always dad's favorite son. Maybe that's because my brother is named after my dad, and maybe because he, unlike myself, chose to spend holidays with my dad after the divorce.

Dennis is the second man my mom married. He is a very kind man. He's the strong quiet type. I've known Dennis for about 19 years now. He and mom married in June of 1989. Dennis is a strong father-figure to John and me. A few years ago mom worked for an airline company, and when the airline closed Mom went to a one-year program of dental assisting while Dennis worked to support our family. She loves her job and currently continues working in this profession. Dennis is a very generous and spirit-filled man and was very patient while mom completed her studies. He and mom are definitely soul mates, very much in love with one another!

Shortly before my parents divorced, my mom left teaching and became a real estate broker to support our family. She later became a loan officer while I was in high school.

The money and the hours were good, but people called mom at home about business at all times of the day and night. Mom always felt that family time is when business shuts down. Mom hated being called at home on business because it intruded on her private family life, and because of this she left the home mortgage business.

6

College

In the Fall of 1989 I enrolled in a local community college. For me, my college years were a time of great inner growth. I grew up as a person and I also expanded my view of the world.

My college years spanned from when I was 18 to 22 years old, which included two years at the community college, two years at a local university and my internship with the local television station.

A friend since my days at the community college, Wendy finds it hard to accept my mental illnesses, but she keeps me in check, sometimes telling me to cut back on my medications when I was perhaps overmedicated.

I was quite popular at the community college. I was a communications chairperson and helped out with the newsletters for the honors fraternity I belonged to.

Part of my schooling was my internship with a local talk show which afforded me the chance to see how a daily live talk show is put on the air and to meet celebrities.

During this time, I learned a lot about the world and that it takes a thick skin —- or a "rubber suit"—to make it in the entertainment business.

I faced a lot of temptations during my college years. It's as if God let go of His "reins" during this time in my life. He let me see what the world believes in and what the center of its desires for many is: money.

Other parts of college years were turbulent for me, more turbulent than if I had walked with the Lord during these four and a half years of my life. I questioned who and what I was sexually during my college years.

Today is a gift. I am so glad to be alive in the 21st Century! I have had a turbulent and yet very loving past, and I have many goals for the future.

I'd like help find a cure for AIDS and travel the world with my family and close friends.

I am schizophrenic and have mild depression and obsessive-compulsive disorder (OCD). I have my crosses to bear. We all have our troubles to take care of, but I am learning to live with this, and feel I am stronger in doing so.

God helps us take care of our troubles. I believe that Christ died for all our sins. This is proven in Isaiah 53:5+6: "He was pierced for our transgressions, He was crushed for our iniquities, the punishment that brought us peace was upon Him, and by His wounds we are healed."

After graduating from a local university, I was in a car accident in the Spring of 1995 which led to a nervous breakdown. Subsequently, I was diagnosed as having schizophrenia, depression and OCD behaviors or traits. To this very day, I am an extremely cautious driver and leery when driving around trucks and bulldozers.

Usually I listen to soul or pop music stations or audio tapes in my car, but the morning of this car accident, which happened when a bulldozer pulled out in front of my car, I was tuned into a Christian radio station. This morning was different.

"Angels are watching over you," a choir sang on the radio. "God is with you."

Moments later, the bulldozer pulled out into my lane of traffic and demolished the right side of my car.

When I graduated from the university I got plugged into a Pre-marital group at my church. I'm expanding this chapter to include some post-graduation experiences I have had while participating in this group for Christians in my age group.

A leader in my church has said that God picks away one layer of our defenses one layer at a time. I believe that right now I'm going through a phase in my life whereby I am growing in faith and being tested for my faith in God.

I realize that I've put up barriers with others, finding it hard to trust others sometimes. God is peeling my layers away, increasing my faith in the Lord.

I think that I'm going through all these phases in my life so that one day I may have a great testimony before the world and the Christian community. I believe that one day the Lord will heal me of my mental illnesses. I will one day be well again. I have faith in God and myself.

I have heard testimonies of people at my church who have overcome many big barriers and troubles in their lives. I hold hope that one day there will be cures for our mental illnesses.

One day all these layers I have built up—defense mechanisms—will all be wiped away and I will have a clean slate. I will be free and I will be full of life!

I date. I broke up with my last "serious" girlfriend in 1996. She wanted to get married after a few months of dating; I didn't want to marry just yet, and so we broke up.

When I was at the local university, I also grappled with what I wanted to do for the rest of my life. I worked for a local newspaper as a news clerk while I was attending the university.

I wrote about 50 news-feature articles and numerous news briefs—as well as daily obituaries, about 20 each day on average—while employed there.

I aspire to write for a living. I helped a local stock broker write a finance book a couple of years after graduating from the local university. I wrote three chapters of the book, which was good experience for me to hone my skills as a writer.

I believe that God has given me the gift of being a writer and a journalist. Every story that I've ever written has always tried to bring out the best in others. I'm a good team player in that way. I always try to highlight the positive to emphasize the good in what is going on.

When I write, whatever I'm writing for or about, I first clear my mind. I think of what I want to say and then make a mental note about what I want to say, and when in my copy I want to say it. In college, my English professors taught us to first write an outline, and then write. But as much as I adore my college English professors, outlines just don't work for me.

I like the words to flow from my head, through my hands and down out through my fingers to the typewriter. I feel more comfortable when I'm writing to let it flow naturally; I can't achieve this with written outlines.

I don't like introductions or conclusions, and when I write I usually just jump right in with the first chapter. After I'm finished writing the basic chapters, then I go back and review what I've written so that I can write the introduction and conclusion.

I am a writer. This is what I love and what I plan to do. In my next chapter, I'll discuss my hopes and desires for the future.

7

Goals

My eyes are looking towards noble and good things. My future looks bright; I have lofty goals and plenty of talent.

Jeremiah 29:11-13 of the Holy Bible says: "For I know the plans I have for you," declares the Lord, "plans to prosper you and not to harm you, plans to give you hope and a future. Then you will call upon me and come and pray to me, and I will listen to you. You will seek me and find me when you seek me with all your heart."

God wants us all to be happy and have bright futures and lofty goals. Goal-setting and dreaming are crucial for a fulfilling life. I believe that there ought to be more dreamers like myself in this world; not only are we refreshing to be around, but we are also leaders.

I have many lofty goals, and if I accomplish them all, I will have lived what I consider to be a very interesting and challenging life.

I am interested in public relations and writing press releases. Maybe one day I will work for a Senator, entertainer, or some major corporation and write their speeches and press releases.

I believe that God will grant each of us the desires of our hearts. Here's what the Holy Bible says in Psalms 37:4: "Delight yourself in the Lord and He will give you the desires of your heart;" I know this is true.

I have realized that God should come first before work. There are no perfect employees, customers or co-workers. For me, my family ranks up there second to God.

I am now stable on my medications, which I have been on for approximately three years. Prior to this, my psychiatrists tried me on various medications until we found the right combinations. I get better and better every day and hopefully one day I will be able to handle a full-time job.

Some people criticize me for trying to reach the top. I can't help but look at these people who don't try to better their lives through education, and what I think about them is that they—not me—are the crazy ones. It's crazy not to try, to my way of thinking. Even for African-Americans—who had wrongly been repressed for years—have the opportunities to achieve higher education if they work towards good grades and pursue a higher education. There's plenty of scholarships and grants so that everyone in this country should have equal access to a higher education.

God plants the seeds in all our heart's desires. God doesn't just randomly put dreams in people's hearts and minds; He intends to help us achieve our heart's desires.

I'd like to get married someday. I'd like to have a family, but due to the fact that mental illness is genetic and hereditary I may opt to adopt children rather than risk spreading my illness onto my biological children.

I would like to leave behind me a legacy that my spouse and children will be able to carry on.

I believe that God gives parents nothing greater than their children. Kids are blessings from above, whether they are adopted or born into a biological family. I want the blessing!

I hope to someday travel the world. If God sees it in my future, there is really no place in this world that I wouldn't want to visit, with the exception of war-zones. Wherever God wills me to go, that's where I shall go.

I'd like to work for a talk show in the future.

8

Amsterdam

After I graduated from the university in the Spring of 1993, my Mom and Dennis paid for me to go to Europe for three weeks! Two good friends who live near me were staying at one of their sister's apartment in Oxford, England. I stayed with them and also with a friend who was an exchange student in high school from Germany.

I took seven rolls of film: three rolls of 36-exposure and four rolls of 24. So that's a lot of pictures! Nearly 200 pictures in all! The trip cost about $1,900 in all, about $80 a day! What a cheap price for a dream come true and the many memories will last me a lifetime!

I gained confidence that I can travel far away from home and take care of myself: I can navigate my way around, meet new people, find places to see and stay at, experience new cultures and people, etc.! A great experience!

I flew into the airport in Amsterdam. Flying into Amsterdam was the cheapest way to fly at the time of my one and only (yet!) trip to Europe!

Once I got to Amsterdam, my German friend met me in the airport. We then went to the Red Light District, which was dark and dank and smelled of pot. I got scared and went to Oxford the next day to stay with my two friends there.

There were lots of American college students in Europe! I found most of the people that I met and encountered to be friendly, courteous and helpful.

My eyes opened up to a lot of new things. I learned a lot about myself and other people. In Amsterdam, for instance, I saw a whole new culture. The natives there were very friendly: in addition to their native Dutch almost all of them spoke English.

In Amsterdam, drugs and prostitution are legal. I saw drugs being sold in restaurants and on the streets. I walked into the Hard Rock Cafe by the Red Light District, and a man was sitting right at the bar when you first walk in, selling drugs. He even had a cardboard price list laying right in front of him on the bar!

Prostitutes are all over the Red Light District. They stand in windows, which have red lights above them. Most of the women are Oriental; my German friend told me that many are married and then sold into prostitution, put on drugs and kept illegally.

I didn't sleep with a prostitute because I believe that God intends sex to be beautiful, natural. I didn't want to pay someone to sleep with me. I believe that prostitution is a misuse of the gift of sex. I didn't do any drugs because I don't believe in them: I believe they're addicting and only harm one's body, mind and spirit.

The people in the Amsterdam Youth Hostel, Bob's Youth Hostel, were friendly! I made a couple of friends there: one guy, John, was from Ireland; a young lady was from Florida; and two guys were from Michigan.

My German friend and another of his friends did drugs in Amsterdam. He wanted to play pool in a dark bar. Drugs scared me. I told my friend that I came all this way from home and was disappointed in him.

The next day I left, via Eurail, for Oxford, England!

That night, I thought about a few things that are noteworthy. I realized that my family was safe and only a thought away. They're part of me and me of them, no matter space or time.

I'm becoming more independent. This is healthy and good. This trip is an act of independence and love. My mind is opening up to new things. I'm seeing new places, people, and cultures. My experiences are expanding, and this is integral to my growth.

At that time, I understood that I'd be back home in less than three weeks! I wanted to see and experience as much as I could at that time and place. Just knowing that I'd be back home in three weeks made me feel secure.

I realize that I doubt myself a lot. I see now that I tell myself a lot that I can't do things like public speaking. Or even like this trip: I used to tell myself that I couldn't go to Europe. Well, I made it! I realize I can either think that I can do something good or I can think I can't do it; either way, I'm right.

On the plane to Amsterdam I sat next to a man. He was an orthopedic surgeon. He took his two daughters and his girlfriend to Amsterdam and France. It was his daughter's first trip to Europe. He gave me some good advice: he told me that everything I need in this life is already inside me.

Daylight had come, and I was on my way to Oxford! On my way there, I passed through rural France via Eurail. I saw a small French city. The land is flat in this region. There are farms and small towns. In one town, the 3 or 4-storied building are made of red brick and have orange-reddish roofs.

From Calais, France, I took a boat over to Dover, England. When I got into Dover, the last train had left for the night and all the hotels were filled so I found a YMCA where I slept on the floor. First thing the next morning, I left for Oxford.

9

Oxford

I had two friends who I stayed with. We lived it up in Oxford! I don't think I had ever drank as much sangria the week I spent in Oxford, which is about 30 minutes from London.

I traveled to Germany on a Eurail pass. On my way, via a Eurail transportation pass, to Germany I passed within three hours of the city of love, Paris! It was timely that I went to Germany because it was my friend's birthday!

I spent six days, from Sunday to Saturday, with George and Chris in Oxford. We went to London one day and saw the Buckingham Palace and the gorgeous parks in the city. We even rode in a caddie!

Most of the time, we looked around Oxford. I took lots of photos. I loved Christ Church! We climbed up a foot tower and saw the entire city from up high!

10

Florence

While I was in Oxford my German friend and another guy spent all their money in Amsterdam, "living it up!" I wanted to see the Swiss Alps and Italy, but my friend was out of money. So alone I took an 18-hour trip via train through the beautiful and breath-taking Swiss Alps and finally got off the train in Florence, Italy.

I didn't make it to Rome because some people I met on the train scared me from going alone: they said that there was too much theft there.

Here's proof-positive that there is a God, or Higher Power: I got off the train and tried to find a hotel. All were booked for the night, I was told. I was tired—you don't sleep well on the trains I was on—and I had no Italian currency. I was tired and hungry. So I stood in line to exchange my money. There was only one female exchanging money. While my German friend was in Amsterdam living it up my first night there before heading for Oxford first thing in the morning, I was in the Youth Hostel we found in Amsterdam. (I highly recommend staying in

Youth Hostels, as they treat you well and feed you.) Anyway, I met two guys, both from Michigan, who were staying in my same Youth Hostel. To my surprise, when I was in line in Florence to change my money, I turned around and those two guys I met in Amsterdam were right behind me! We eventually exchanged our money, got a hotel for the night and then ate. What a miracle that I would run into these guys who helped me so much!

Florence is a beautiful place! At night people stand around and talk while drinking wine. There is such a unique ambiance to Florence, which is rich in culture including historic landmarks and artistic works by famous artists such as Michalangelo and his world-renown David sculpture.

Sitting in this big circle, surrounded by historic buildings, I could feel my spirit soar just a few feet above me. I got scared and my "spirit" came back inside me. I had never experienced anything like this before. I didn't know if I was having an out-of-body experience or just losing my mind, but when it happened I got scared quickly and my "spirit" promptly came back inside me.

I'd like to visit Florence again in the future. It will be interesting to see how my views of my favorite spot in Europe—Florence—may change due to the grace of maturity.

11

Germany

After visiting Florence, I took the Eurail back to Germany to see my friend on his birthday! I was fortunate to catch the Andy Warhol exhibit. One neat thing about Germany is that they rent out CD's like we do videos here in the States!

My German friend had his sister and elderly grandparents over to his apartment for a little birthday party. He served Danish pastries and coffee, and we all sat around a coffee table.

Later that night, my friend threw a party to welcome me to Germany! His friends from college came over to his place and stayed until late in the night. They were eager to hear all about my customs, schools, and hobbies.

My friend belonged to a group of the more radical students in his hometown. They all were very unique. My friend and I took in a breakfast overlooking the downtown and ate bratwurst one night in town.

Shopping in Germany is very unique. The mall we went to was actually outside! There were many shops outside the mall. Bikes were a popular mode of transportation around town for many of those German folk.

12

God 2

God created each of us. If not for God, none of us would even be here to begin with. It is God who loves and nurtures each of us, His children.

God is the center of my universe. In my world, God comes first—before myself, my family, my work and my friends. God comes first.

I think that if more people put their faith in God then we would have a much stronger and better world for us all to live in.

Don't get me wrong here. God wants us to work hard, prosper and love our loved ones with all our hearts, but God also said not to put any idols before him. I'm guilty here, since I have idolized rock stars.

Idols come in many different shapes and sizes. Money is an idol to many people. Family members can also be idols. For some, just traveling around the world—searching in the wrong places for something greater than themselves—is their idol.

It is good and praiseworthy to seek riches, fame and health, but those things should never come before God.

One appropriate Scripture is: "Finally, brothers, whatever is true, whatever is noble, whatever is right, whatever is pure, whatever is lovely, whatever is admirable—if there is anything excellent or praiseworthy—think on these things. Whatever you have learned or received or heard from me, or seen in me—put into practice. And the God of peace will be with you." That's from Philippines, chapter four and verses eight and nine.

If you think and pray about it, it becomes clear that the word whatever may be replaced with the word God in the above Scripture, for God is true, God is noble and God is right and pure, etc.

I love God, truly, with all my heart. God gave His begotten son, Jesus, to die on the cross for all of our sins. We may all be freed from our sins if we would only ask the Lord into our hearts.

The Holy Bible says, and I believe, that one must be born again to enter the kingdom of God. It can be as simple as sincerely asking God into one's heart, to wash away our sins in this world and start anew.

Here's my prayer to become saved, or born again: "Dear God, I am a sinner and I have lived a sinful life up until now. Please come into my heart and cleanse my spirit. I realize that my soul will be saved now, and will remain the same from this day forward."

We live in an age of Grace. There is much cruelty and sin in our world today. I have heard more than one preacher say that we live in a time of great sin and Grace.

By Grace, I mean that God is eager and ready to forgive each of us for our sins. God wants us all to live Holy lives. Treating each person we encounter as each of us would want to be treated is the noble and upright way to live.

God has saved me from myself and from many awful situations in my life. Even when I was the scum of the Earth and living in sin, God reached down and grabbed me by the throat and lifted me back up.

Whenever I turned my back on God—especially during my tumultuous teen-age years—God has always been faithful and "there" for me. God has always been walking beside me, "carrying" me at certain times.

God is faithful. God is a loving and caring and thoughtful God. God only gives us as much as we can handle. When God sent me to the mental institution, I was down on my knees and closest to God at that time, and yet God didn't put anything in my path there that I wasn't able to deal with, despite the fact that I flipped out in thinking that people there were trying to kill me.

It is by the Grace of God that I survived being in a mental institution when I thought that I would be killed in there. God has been with me through thick and thin, as you can ascertain through my writing.

Men will let you down. Friends, family, neighbors, co-workers and all people for that matter, they all let you down sooner or later, whether intentionally or unintentionally. But God is a faithful God who will always be there for each of us.

Another Scripture that I would like to share with you, the reader of this book, comes from the Book of Jeremiah, chapter 29 and verses 11 through 13: "For I know the plans I have for you," declares the Lord, "plans to prosper you and not to harm you, plans to give you hope and a future. Then you will call upon me and come and pray to me, and I will listen to you. You will seek me and find me when you seek me with all your heart."

What a beautiful Scripture. These words remind me of my potential, and all I have to contribute to society. I have a heart of gold, a healthy work ethic and a strong will; a powerful combination that will help me to succeed in helping to make our world a happier Earth.

The Holy Bible also says that God will grant each of our hearts' desires. I believe that God will someday grant me my desire to work for a talk show.

God will get me through the changing of my medicines for my mental illnesses. I am stable now for three years on my current medications. I believe that someday I will emerge without having to take any more medications; our medical research is progressing at an astounding rate in most areas of science.

In 1996 I was baptized in the Holy Spirit. I was water baptized, fully submerged in water so that I may grow closer to God, the Lord and my church congregation.

Recently, I had elders at the interdenominational church that I attend pray for my healing. I asked for physical and mental healing. The elders prayed for me, and towards the end of their prayer, I collapsed. An elder behind me caught me and broke my fall.

What this means is that I believe I will be healed, slowly, of my mental illnesses. I have faith that this healing will come to me.

Everything happens in God's own time, once you turn your life over to the Lord. My grandfather always told me that God works miracles slowly in people's lives. My grandfather, whom I lovingly called ''Gramps,'' has since passed but his legacy hasn't.

I am in a mode by which I am getting rooted in the Lord's teachings and His Word.

With all of my problems—and my problems, I realize, are minuscule compared to other people's suffering as in third world countries—I could be wallowing in my tear drops. But instead, I praise the Lord and God with all my heart.

When you are most down, that's when you need to put praise worship music into your CD or cassette player. We need to worship the Lord in all our ways. When we are down, inspirational Christian music will lift us up. We also need to make the Holy Bible a companion in our lives; we must read the Holy Bible daily to stay ''plugged in'' to the Word.

God could easily be a cruel God who shames and condemns His children; but instead, God loves each of us very much and He blesses each of us every day.

Many of us dismiss everyday miracles as being nothing at all. But there is a natural progression of growth out there, and inside each of us.

We all have heard others say that when they look back on their lives that they have 20/20 vision. It's only while we are in the present that things don't always make sense to us. But in the long-run, at the end of our tunnels, things make sense to us. This is God's way of working in our lives, and revealing this to us.

When we seek God with all of our hearts, He rewards each of us completely. God will be there for each of us when we seek Him.

For me, faith is the hard part of religion, of believing in God and entrusting our lives in his hands. I always tried to do things for myself. I guess that some of this mental training came from being a Boy Scout. Boy Scouts are trained, sensibly and responsibly, to pay their own way, to be independent.

Therefore, I have difficulty giving all my hopes, worries and problems to the Lord. It's hard to give these things to a higher power, to the Lord.

As I walk closer to God, the easier it is for me to give everything in my life to Him. But I do understand what it's like for many people to give their complete faith in the Lord, because I have been just like these very people.

I must have faith that someday there will be cures for AIDS and cancer, and that I will continue to get better on my medications and eventually have the opportunities to travel the world over.

God is always with us. Just like it is said in the Footprints plaque I hung on my wall at home, the Lord carries us when we are the weakest. That's when only one set of footprints—God's footprints—are found in the sand.

When we are most needy, that's when we don't see two footprints in the sand, only one set of footprints. That's God's footprints in the sand that we see.

I hope that each of you reading my book will be able to give the glory and the honor and the tribulations of your lives to the Lord. There is nothing greater—no greater feeling or sensation—than that of being completely in God's Will.

God has a plan for each of our lives. If we only listen to Him and are led by peace, then we will be closest to God. This is no race and there is no competition out there. We each have our own race—our own true destiny—to live by.

We all must remain ''in touch'' with God's Will for our lives; this applies to everybody, no matter who we are in stature in this materialistic world we live in.

We each are unique beings that must follow our instincts and our goals to prosper and leave behind a lasting legacy of love and kindness.

God is with all of us, all of the time. This is something that must be remembered by believers and non-believers alike. God is faithful. God is with us through thick and thin, even when we are living in sin. God is only a prayer away for redemption.

For some people, it is required that they fall to their knees—literally—before they see the ''light'' and accept the Lord into their hearts.

I heard a testimony from a Christian who testified about how he came to God. He was walking in sinful ways during the hippie movement when he tried to kill himself and found the Lord in the hospital.

My testimony of how I came to know the Lord may not be as radical as my friend's. I was saved with God when I was much younger. God came into my life and made clear that I should have no idols before the Lord.

God remains faithful to me when I wasn't always faithful to Him. May each of you walk every day of your lives with the Lord.

There is no greater feeling than that of believing and knowing that the Lord is right here for and with you always.

I pray every night: ''Dear Lord Jesus, God and the Holy Spirit. It is my prayer this evening and always that: Our heavenly Father, who art in heaven, hollowed be thy name. Thy kingdom come, they will be done, on Earth as it is in heaven. Give us this day our daily bread and forgive us of our trespasses as we forgive those who trespass against us. And lead us not into temptation but deliver us from evil, for thine is the power, kingdom and glory, forever and ever, amen."

I also pray every night that my dad will be cured of lung cancer, the cure for AIDS will be found and made public and that my family and I live into our 80's and older!

I have been praying these prayers for at least several years now. Watch out, what you pray for something, because once you do, I have found that when we pray for better lives for ourselves and others God moves quickly and takes us up on these prayers! So be prepared for God to work great things in your life when you pray!

13

OCD/Schizophrenia

I live with schizophrenia. Some consider this to be a terrible thing to have to live with. I am coming to accept the fact that I am schizophrenic and will have to take medications to fight this disorder—just as diabetics do—for the rest of my life.

I had been seeing a counselor for about three months prior to my landing in a local mental health hospital.

My counselor had set up an appointment for me to see a psychiatrist; the appointment was for one week after I went into a local mental health hospital.

Up until this point, I had worked part-time at a local call center, which was very accommodating of my hospitalization; my job was waiting for me there as soon as I was well enough to work.

I was put on medications to control the dopamine in my blood. I had learned from reading books about achieving one's dreams that I have to become obsessed with attaining my goals, as long as I wasn't hurting myself or others. I now have to ''re-train'' my brain from that dysfunctional way of thinking.

Dopamine is a chemical produced in the brain and functions much like adrenaline. Before being treated with medications, my face turned red and got bloated when I obsessed about things. The dopamine—my chemical imbalance—was working me over in a bad way!

The medications I'm currently taking have ceased—hopefully for always—these and other symptoms I experienced when I wasn't taking the proper medications.

I start getting very paranoid feelings that people are out to kill or hurt me or my family members when I'm not taking my prescribed medications.

I have learned from talking with consumers of medications that whenever they went off their meds they landed back into the hospital. I take my medications faithfully; I never want to return to a mental institution.

Never have I hallucinated or heard voices. My diagnosis is paranoid schizophrenic. I fear that one day my prognosis will worsen and I'll begin to hear voices and see images or smell things that aren't really there.

Paranoid thoughts are one thing to handle, but hallucinations are more difficult—to my thinking—to bear on one's shoulders.

I'm taking the generic of Clozaril, Clozapine, and Navane to control my paranoia. I've taken a handful of different anti-psychotic drugs before my doctors found the right combination of medications for me to control my symptoms.

When I left a local mental health hospital, I was given some medicine to take. Later that same week I began to see a psychiatrist at a county-funded mental health services center.

I was prescribed one medicine and then another until we found the right medications for me—three psychiatrists later!

Being diagnosed with paranoid schizophrenic and OCD, I have learned to live each day to its fullest. My disorders could worsen and so I just want to walk in the Lord's Will for my happy, productive life.

I still get some "normal" paranoid thoughts, such as getting mugged when alone in a city's back alley or someone freaking out and beating me up. For the most part, however, these paranoid thoughts are appropriate to the situations in which I find myself.

Persons with OCD are most commonly identified because they wash their hands 100 times a day or check 10 times to make sure the oven is turned off or the front door locked.

For healthy persons, this is ludicrous behavior, but for the OCD sufferer, their reality is ritualistic and painful.

My OCD centers around my compulsive observing of famous people. I want to be famous someday and so I watch and study famous entertainers and pay close attention to their talents and what they have to say about their famous talents and worlds around them.

Thanks to God and Luvox, a new medication for OCD sufferers, I am able to live a rather normal life without obsessing on this or that.

With Luvox, I can manage my life and lead a normal life. I take 100 mg three times a day of Luvox. It helps me tremendously to control obsessive thoughts. Now I only have an obsessive-type of thought every once in awhile, in what would be considered a normal and healthy type.

I still get paranoid, OCD-type fearful thoughts that some people would want to hurt me or my family and close friends. With medications, too, these thoughts come
only once in awhile.

OCD itself fascinates me. Schizophrenia is an illness—and so is OCD—but it's more fun to write about OCD than schizophrenia. The reasons behind this are simple.

As a schizophrenic patient, I take my medications and think positive thoughts and the paranoia is greatly under control. I must add here that a healthy work environment and the support of medications, loving people in my life and the many medications I take have enabled me to reach a "stable" life. If any of these combinations were to be altered or taken away I'm certain I would be in a mental institution. I rely heavily on my medications and support system in place in my life today.

With OCD, however, I think about interesting things and persons, such as family members and celebrities. This is fun, when I'm having positive, uplifting thoughts. Luvox and cognitive thinking techniques also help cut down tremendously on my obsessions.

My third psychiatrist put me on Paxil, an anti-depressant, to control my OCD. Paxil is a very good drug, but isn't powerful enough to reduce my symptoms.

Psychiatry is a very tricky business. It's all about trial and error, and is like shooting darts in the dark, never knowing if it's a hit or miss until you try out the different drugs with hopes that the consumer's symptoms are reduced.

It usually takes a month or so for medications to really get into the bloodstream, thus making it hard to be sure whether or not a particular drug works or not.

As I write about my trials and tribulations, I just want to stop right here and thank Jesus, who shed His blood on the cross to bear all our sins. I have so much love and respect for our Lord.

I am feeling—at this very moment—tremendously grateful to the Lord for allowing me to share my writing gift and my recollections of my life and its problems today with you, my readers. This book is my gift—inspired by God—to the world.

Lucky for me, my fourth psychiatrist had the proper insight to put me on Luvox for OCD. As with most medicines, it's trial and error. Sometimes medications will work only for a short period of time or not at all.

This isn't my case. I took to Luvox right from the beginning. The drug helps me to think more clearly and to have healthier thought patterns with a low level of obsessive content.

I read a really good book, which I highly recommend to loved ones and OCD patients, called Brain Lock. In this book, J. Schwartz, the author, teaches readers how to change their lives by changing the way they think.

OCD persons are instructed to think about other things whenever an obsessive thought pops up.

It has been proven that the brains of OCD persons are shaped differently from those of healthy individuals. Schwartz's cognitive therapy can actually change the brain chemistry back to its initial, healthy form!

Other drugs used to treat OCD include: Anafranil, Prozac and Zoloft.

There are many prescription drugs available to today's schizophrenic consumer. Zyprexa, more commonly known as Olanzapine, is one very effective anti-psychotic drug.

Clozaril, equally-effective to Zyprexa in terms of controlling psychoses, requires a bi-weekly white blood cell level lab test.

Roughly one in 1,000 consumers of Clozaril have white blood levels that drop to dangerously low levels, and therefore the bi-weekly tests help to monitor this drug treatment of schizophrenia. Actually, Clozaril recipients have to go weekly blood draws the first six months of taking the drug to monitor white blood cells which are prone to fall—if ever—during the first several months of taking Clozaril.

There is much hope out there for those concerned about schizophrenia and OCD. The National Alliance for Research on Schizophrenia and Depression (NARSAD) has a quarterly newsletter which outlines its funding of $53.1 million in grants to 759 scientists at 117 universities and medical centers.

In their winter supplement for 1997, NARSAD reported a correlation between schizophrenia and smoking.

Persons with schizophrenia have been found to have a deficiency of nicotinic receptors in the hippocampus, a place in the brain that is responsible for memory formation and sensory stimuli.

The nicotine in smoking, researchers have found, balances this deficiency in sensory gating, also known as screening out repeated stimuli.

I opened this section of my book by writing that I am coming to accept my mental illnesses and having to take medications for the remainder of my life.

Forgiving God and coming to God are two separate issues, both of which I've had to come to terms with facing OCD and schizophrenia in my life.

When I returned home from a local mental health hospital in March of 1995, I was too tired from all the new medications they gave me while I was there to do too much of anything but get a good night's rest, which is what I did.

Somehow everything in my life leading up to this single moment when I got back home from the hospital seemed to be telling me: I am now a grown-up. Dennis tells me: "You're no longer a kid."

I was a changed man from this experience: spiritually, physically and mentally. I will forever be changed from going to a local mental health hospital.

Spiritually, I drew closer to God in the hospital, closer than I have ever come to God.

I believe that we each have to come to that breaking point in our lives when we realize that we aren't big enough to handle it all. This is when we come to God, asking God into our hearts to save us from our sins.

I had "come" to God as a youngster at my grandma Ruth's church, but this time it meant more to me. I was old enough to appreciate this gift from God, the gift of redemption. God is love and welcomes us when we ask Him to. It's that clear.

Physically, my brain is "digesting" mind-altering drugs that are helping my disorders stay under control.

Mentally—and this may sound minuscule to some but it really isn't—I've learned to have discipline and be organized. I take certain medicines three times a day and all the rest at bedtime.

Shortly after my release from the hospital, I began to see all these weird people walking around. In the malls, at local restaurants, everywhere.

They weren't weird, just normal people with normal problems. What changed was my viewpoint, having just been released from a mental institution.

The people in our malls and restaurants looked just like me and most everyone I met in the hospital (with the exception of patients who drool).

It's hard to imagine how many people out there need psychological and psychiatric help but aren't getting help.

There is still stigma against the mentally ill, but things are improving. Employers may no longer ask applicants if they are mentally ill and must provide accommodations to help them in the workplace.

No one "looks" mentally ill. Most mentally ill people I have met look just like the "normal" next guy.

Living with OCD and schizophrenia is manageable in today's world. But just a couple of decades ago there was little anyone could do for people with mental illness except hospitalize them for life.

Scientists now believe genetics are one of the causes of schizophrenia. Gene therapy may provide some answers in the fight against schizophrenia.

Still, much more research needs to be done before cures for OCD and schizophrenia are found. It is my prayer that this will one day occur.

Let's pray: "Dear Lord Jesus, God and the Holy Spirit, it is our prayer today and always that improved treatments and eventually cures will be found for OCD and schizophrenia. Thank you."

14

Therapy

We all have our trials and tribulations. Some of us go through different periods sooner or later than others. Some may appear to "have it all together," but I'm sure even the finest public speakers get at least a little nervous before speaking.

I need help to get me over the hills and mountains in my life. No one, I realize, makes it on their own volition. It's not easy to admit that one needs help.

I call it "coming to God" when people decide to turn things over to the Lord rather than trying to hold onto and control every aspect of their life, which just can't be done.

I suppose that you can call reaching out for psychological and/or psychiatric help "coming to therapy."

I realize that if not for the medicines in my life, I'd be in dire straits. I've found that the medicine isn't an end to it all. My medicines are like my water-wings.

Like making it in this world, no one makes it on their own and we all need help. For me, I need therapy to almost the same degree that I need my medications to get me through the day.

Shortly before my nervous breakdown I started seeing a counselor. I was seeing this counselor once a week; in retrospect, twice each week may have been beneficial, although my counselor had a heavy case load.

He helped me with issues such as taking my medications, working to increase my self-esteem and just getting by day-by-day. We didn't get that much into my painful past.

A few days every week I volunteer at a local hospital. I work in the marketing department. I help them write press releases. Everyone is very friendly and understanding of my mental illnesses there!

When my counselor had done all he could for me—doing his very best to get me Medicaid, Medicare and Social Security benefits—he then turned my case over to a terrific day-treatment program where I was going for counseling.

The program has a director, a cooking and sewing instructor and four counselors. The social workers teach cooking and run group therapy and classes on self-esteem, psychological education and assertiveness training.

The program's director is a great guy who is always smiling and calls every person by their first name. This makes us all feel special.

I have four counselors at the day treatment program I go to three mornings every week. I have my own counselor of the four who I communicate my feelings and problems to.

My counselor teaches my group therapy class on Fridays. Other classes taught at the day treatment program include: wellness, cooking, managing your symptoms, anger, stress management, psychological education, drama, humor, current events, anxiety and assertiveness.

I tried the cooking class for about a month, but then felt that I needed more group therapy and so I went back to going to group therapy more than once per day.

While in the cooking class, I learned how to make chicken cacciatore and salmon patties with lemon-cheese sauce, and came across a to-die-for salad dressing recipe!

Here it is: 1 cup salad oil, 1/2 cup sugar, 1/3 cup cider vinegar (brown), two tablespoons onion (grated) and two teaspoons of Worcestershire sauce. Mix all the dressing ingredients in a blender all at one time. Enjoy!

When I started day treatment in July of 1996, I learned quickly that because my foot tingles doesn't mean that people are out to get my mom, and I learned that the tingling on the side of my head didn't mean that I was in danger. What a relief! It's no fun walking around thinking people are out to kill myself or my beloved mom!

I realize now that the weather man and news persons aren't talking to me, which I once thought about people at the local television station where I had interned. I thought that these media persons were talking to and about me. My medications and discipline of not watching a lot of local news are helping to subside my illogical reasoning to see reality for what it is.

As for the media talking to me through the local news, intensive therapy has made me see the reality that they're not talking to me directly at all.

Everything discussed in group therapy is held strictly confidential. We have a group leader—a social worker or counselor—who keeps the group on track.

Group therapy has helped me to put a mirror—so-to-speak —up to my obsessive and psychotic thoughts and see the reality of the situation.

I have delusional thoughts. Then these thoughts have become obsessive. Therapy has helped me to realize that no one is out to get my family, friends or myself.

In psychological education class, I learned about all kinds of mental illness—manic depression, bipolar, OCD and the different types of schizophrenia.

I've learned about medications as they have been prescribed from the earliest breakthroughs in medical research or mental illnesses to today's sophisticated medications.

There is yet to be found a cure for schizophrenia although NARSAD is investing millions of dollars every year in scientists around the country for research for even better treatments and possibly a cure.

Once every week I see my therapist. We talk for about 45 minutes about what's going on in my life since we met the week before.

This intensive therapy is teaching me coping skills which I desperately need to survive in this competitive and fast-paced world; having schizophrenia and OCD together makes more difficult.

My thoughts tend to scatter all over the place. My psychologist told me that this is part of my schizophrenia.

My psychiatrist, who I see about once every three months, prescribes for me the "miracle drug," Clozaril. This medication, accompanied with Navane, has worked wonders for me as I walk towards mental health.

I have my blood tested once every other week because there is a risk in taking Clozaril: your white blood cells can drop drastically and rather quickly.

I'm taking Luvox for my OCD. Never before have I felt better and more in-control of my life since I was a child; I believe I've been suffering with OCD since I was about 10 years old, when my parents divorced.

My OCD was a coping mechanism back then, a control issue.

My mental illnesses, especially my schizophrenia, are mysterious to me. Each and every day I—and researchers across the world—discover new aspects to this disease.

For instance, I learned in group therapy that there is no treatment for the paranoia that comes with having paranoid schizophrenia. Currently, researchers have found medicines that only treat delusions and hallucinations.

I am committing myself to learning more about my illnesses. I am doing this by reading about my illnesses and talking with people—

such as my psychiatrist and psychologist—who are knowledgeable about them.

My therapist and psychiatrist have told me that I will have to take my medications for the rest of my life. How do I feel about this?

I have ambivalent feelings about taking my medication as prescribed.

On one hand, the meds I'm taking are helping me live a "normal," productive life. On the other hand, taking meds at specific times requires a great deal of care for one's improved mental health and discipline to take the meds on time.

I have made my peace with God in regards to my having to take medications every day of my life.

Most of the consumers I have talked to have told me that the reason why they land themselves in the hospital is that they stopped taking their medications.

I fear going to the hospital, as do most people with mental illness. Fortunately for me, if I do have to go to the hospital, I have insurance and can now go to hospital-run mental illness wards and this makes me feel optimistic that I won't have to go back into the hospital I first went in, and this makes me feel secure in that I know I will get terrific care in the hospital I'd be sent to.

15

Family and Friends' Support

No one makes it on his own, especially if you have OCD and schizophrenia. I learned this quickly from talking with other mentally ill people in the hospital.

Support comes in many shapes and sizes—sometimes solicited and sometimes a random gift—and we all need it.

Support groups, one-on-one therapy, friends and families provide excellent support in the most fortunate of all the cases.

I am blessed. My family and friends have been, without fault, very supportive of me as I battle my mental illnesses.

When I was in the hospital, my mom, grandfather, grandmother Ruth, Dennis and my good friend Lisa came to visit me.

Many people with mental illnesses are shunned by their family and even friends. I've been fortunate; I have a strong support system of family and friends in place that helps me tremendously.

My psychologist and psychiatrist help me tremendously. They have opened my eyes to see reality vs. delusions. Battling mental illness is a constant struggle. It's almost like mind over matter in some less severe cases. Unfortunately, I'm not one of these cases.

I am always on the "alert," watching out to make sure people won't hurt me or my beloved and supportive family.

It's a paradox: the more supportive my family and friends are towards me, the closer I draw to them, and the more I love them, the more I fear that they'll get killed or hurt by others. I guess this means that I care for my family and friends.

My brother is a great source of support. Although my brother lives far away, we remain close emotionally. We have a very strong bond and a connection that runs very deep.

John—my brother named after my father and grandfather—is two and a half years older than me. My "big brother" looks out for me and has my best interests at heart.

My mom is a source of constant support. I love my mom dearly. Mom has always encouraged me to do my very best—in school and with friendships and family. That's all anyone can ask for: that they do their very best at all times. "Even if you fail, at least you tried," Mom says.

I was born six weeks pre-mature. The doctor arrived late, and my Mom almost died giving birth to me, her second and last child.

Mom is a giving, caring, warm-hearted, highly-esteemed person. She's someone who's always there for you when you're in need.

Dennis never complains about anything or anyone. I've never met anyone with an attitude as positive as Dennis'.

My dad is the type of father who tries to be perfect: he remembers birthdays, holidays and is a good listener. I just don't see my father enough. My dad has always cared for me but in past years he must have found it hard to express his love for me to me. He now lives far away from me in actual miles, but our relationship is based on stone now. He is one of my main sources of support today. We talk long-distance on the phone every week.

About six months ago my dad was diagnosed with lung cancer, and three days a week he goes to the hospital for intense chemotherapy. Then for the next 27 days he's off the medicine and feels great! I have a strong conviction that my dad will pull out of his cancer. The doctors have told him it isn't spreading, which is wonderful news.

My room-mate of three years now is also schizophrenic. He's a daily source of support.

Some days I come home feeling "beat" and he just lets me go to my room and turn on some music or go to bed. He respects my need to spend some time—roughly one hour—alone every day.

My room-mate and I have cook-outs, go for walks and go to parties together. He studies hard for his second bachelor's degree, the first in accounting and the second in psychology. He wants to become a case manager for the day treatment program I attended for two years. I appreciate my friend being around as my room-mate and I also enjoy those brief moments when we're apart; I treasure solitude in moderation.

Grandpa shows his love to me the way he knows best: he gives me food! I have stuffed shelves, refrigerator and freezer thanks to grandpa! Grandpa likes to give me food! Lots of food!

My grandpa keeps to himself often—he comes over to my parents' house for dinner every Sunday evening. It's always nice to see him!

My grandma Ruth remarried four years ago to Fred. They are long-distance support and are understanding of my mental illnesses.

We recently received Juno, a free E-Mail service for personal computers. Mom, Dennis and I can now E-Mail my grandma Ruth, John and my cousins and aunt and uncle!

Family and friends can be a blessing in one's life. For me, this is true: I have been blessed with the close support that I find in my family and a handful of close friends.

16

Benefits

Acquiring one's Social Security Disability (SSDI) checks is difficult and challenging, but worthwhile!

Before being accepted, I had three hearings to go through. The third time around I hired an attorney who specializes in SSDI benefits.

I had to go before a judge. I was so nervous! My attorney asked me questions, which I answered honestly.

My psychiatrist, counselor and rehabilitation vocational counselor all wrote letters saying that I'm not up for working at this time due to my mental illnesses.

It took from the beginning when I first applied for benefits in March of 1995 until January of 1997 before I was awarded SSDI checks.

In the meantime, all doctor visits and medications came out of my parents' pockets. Therapy and medications are very expensive. Towards the end of last year—just about two months before getting my SSDI award—my vocational rehabilitation paid for my medicine.

After my SSDI award, I went to see a case worker so that I could obtain a state program that pays for consumers' medications.

Two years after I received the state assistance I was awarded Medicare. Once on Medicare, I can earn more than $700 per month for a total of nine months without losing my benefits. For many, volunteerism is a great way to go in order to work for no pay without losing one's benefits and feeling productive at the same time. I choose to volunteer for a local publication so that I can work and not lose my benefits, as I am not paid for work with my volunteer job.

While I'm unable to work for money, at least I'm volunteering at a local publication and am building my skills so that when I do work for money I can go back into the work force with transferable skills to offer my prospective employers.

17

Self-Image

I've always struggled with low self-esteem.

My self-image is getting better every day, and my trust that there will one day be a cure for schizophrenia gives me great hope.

People with mental illnesses are often told—or worse yet tell themselves—that they are different or rejects in society.

I've tried to stay away from labeling myself mentally ill. I didn't wish for this; I was born genetically with schizophrenia.

I believe my OCD was mostly learned, but then again I have that stubborn German/Swedish pride inside me. That German stubborn hold onto an idea to the point of obsession may very well be the German in me; my OCD may be genetic like my schizophrenia.

Growing up being ridiculed by my peers who called me "gay" was tough to swallow. From the age of 10 and all through high school I was called gay.

I have nothing against gay persons; some of my closest friends are gay.

But when you're not sure what to think when puberty hits, it was even harder to deal with my sexuality when persons were calling me gay every day.

My self-esteem was very low all through school. I have never—repeat, NEVER —- gotten into any sort of physical fist fights in my life. I still feared older and bigger and hateful students.

In college, my self-esteem still wavered greatly. The scars from high school run deeply and are hard to forget.

For me, public speaking 101 was murder. My pulse raced and I became clammy. I hated speaking publicly, until I actually got up there and did it.

I understand that public speaking is one of the greatest of human fears. The more I did it, the calmer and more poised I became. A public speaking class I took helped me to enjoy public speaking—and "un-learn" my fear.

I was jobless for about six months after college before I got my first as a job free-lance writer for a local monthly newspaper.

I love to write. Nothing compares to writing!

I believe that faith has a lot to do with one's self-esteem. Since as far as I can remember back, I have always loved the Lord.

My parents took my brother and me to a Lutheran church when we were growing up. I recall playing the part of Jesus in the Christmas play.

I had friends early on in my church life. I have friends in my current church, a non-denominational church.

I have always enjoyed going to church. For me, church wasn't something that my parents or pastors rammed down my throat. In high school, I was skeptical of my religious beliefs. I think it's healthy for everyone to form his own beliefs. This, I have found, actually deepens one's faith, as this questioning did for me.

Church was a fascinating thing to explore for me as a child. Church and God and Jesus up on the cross and all of these Biblical heroes enthralled me.

To this day, I love going to church and reading the Holy Bible.

I date. I'm currently dating a girl, Melissa, who is 27 years old. She fits the perfect image that I look for in a girl: 5' 10" (I'm 6'5"), with beautiful blue eyes and a wonderful personality. She's warm, considerate, thoughtful, gentle and kind.

I dated a different girl, June, in 1996 for about five months. She and I did lots of fun things together. She kept a memoir scrapbook of the things we did together. Restaurant napkins, pictures, flowers and Scriptures made up our journal.

I like to exercise, go roller blading, swimming, jogging and lifting weights. These are healthy hobbies of mine. Exercising is a self-esteem booster.

18

Mid-20's

Sometimes what we go through is too painful for us to see why this is happening to us. Hindsight makes it easier to understand and accept our tribulations.

We want things to go our way, and we want to have everything done as we'd like them to be done. Here's a poem that may help each of us to see how God wants us to see things relevant to our lives:

"God grant me the serenity to accept the things I cannot change, Courage to change the things I can, and the wisdom to know the difference. Living one day at a time; enjoying one moment at a time; accepting hardship as the pathway to peace.

Taking, as He did, this sinful world as it is, not as I would have it; trusting that He will make all things right if I surrender to His will; that I may be reasonably happy in this life, and supremely happy with him forever in the next."

These words ring true and best sum the above poem: "Live each day to its fullest." God is always with each and every one of us, and sometimes we tend to forget this because we are in the midst of confusion, trials and tribulations.

We sometimes let doubt creep in, forgetting that the God who created us loves us always and unconditionally.

Often we try to control situations in our lives, rather than surrender them to God. Ultimately, God is in control, for He has a plan for all of our lives.

When faced with trials and tribulations, it's important to remember that God may be testing us but He is always with us. I believe God wants us to live in the present. He wants us to learn from and enjoy memories of the past and He wants us to plan for a fruitful future, but mostly, I believe, God wants us to live in the present moment.

"Do not be anxious about anything, but in everything, by prayer and petition, with thanksgiving, present your requests to God. And the peace of God, which transcends all understanding, will guard your hearts and your minds in Christ Jesus.

God wants to bring our desires and burdens to Him, and He'll take care of them for us. There is no need to be anxious or fearful, for God is always with us.

We, as servants to Christ, are to think of happy, positive and excellent things.

The following Scripture offers encouragement and safety in our trouble world. Jeremiah 1:19: "They will fight against you but will not overcome you, for I am with you and will rescue you,' declares the Lord."

Before I bought my condo in 1999, my room-mate and I lived in an apartment complex for the mentally ill. I lived seven miles from my mother and her husband's home.

My room-mate has a black and white cat. I'm going along with the idea, but I prefer dogs. Cats can be impersonal and don't like to be touched. Dogs, on the other hand, like to be around people.

I go to therapy once a week with my counselor. We talk for almost an hour about my past, my present problems and goals for the future.

Since my breakdown in March of 1995, I feel that I have grown a great deal.

Today, I am more considerate and compassionate for others. I realize that there are many others out there that are worse off than I am.

I am thankful to God that there are sophisticated and helpful drugs on the market now that battle schizophrenia and OCD. Just a few years ago, there was little one could do to combat schizophrenia except take some rather ineffective drugs from neurologists. Not many years ago, I would have been institutionalized because there weren't effective drugs available.

I no longer take people for granted. I realize that we are all special and have unique, God-given talents that—when used—makes us all productive members of society. My talents are in writing, and I use them often in my various volunteer jobs.

I understand now what it must be like to be a parent. I've learned love from my parents; I have learned to love myself more because of my parents' support of me.

I'm not sure whether I want to have children of my own or not. It is costly and demanding to have children, and I don't want to pass my mental illnesses onto my children, although much better treatments for mental illness surely will be available when they grow up.

I never want to return to a mental institution; it's a scary place to be. In mental institutions, you have very little control and can leave only when they feel you are ready. I take my medications faithfully and on time every day to prevent another nervous breakdown.

I ask God to show me His will. There is nothing I want today more than to love the Lord and follow His path for my life. A Scripture from Psalms 25:4-5 is my daily prayer: "Show my your ways, O Lord, teach me your paths; guide me in your truth and teach me, for you are God my Savior, and my hope is in you all day long."

When we put our trust in God, something miraculous happens: we begin to feel better! God has everything under control; sometimes we just don't want to believe it. We want to think we can control events in our lives by ourselves.

I go to a non-denominational church and attend a group for believers my age. It's good to have fellowship with other Christian believers my age.

The church I go to accepts persons of all faiths. We're not Lutheran or Catholic per se, although there are many Lutherans and Catholics that attend the church I go to.

19

Future

As we each face the unknown of our futures, we may walk in peace by knowing that God is always there for us. "Footprints" sums this up best:

"One night a man had a dream. He dreamed he was walking along the beach with the Lord. Across the sky flashed scenes from his life. For each scene, he notices two sets of footprints in the sand: one belonged to him, and the other to the Lord. When the last scene of his life flashed before him, he looked back at the footprints in the sand. He noticed that many times along the path of his life there was only one set of footprints. He also noticed that it happened at the very lowest and saddest times in his life.

This really bothered him, and he questioned the Lord about it.

'Lord, You said that once I decided to follow You, You'd walk with me all the way. But I have noticed that during the most troublesome times in my life, there is only one set of footprints and I don't understand why when I needed you most you would leave me.'

The Lord replied, 'My precious child, I love you and would never leave you. During your times of trial and suffering, when you see only one set of footprints, it was then that I carried you.'"

The author of "Footprints" is unknown, but surely the author's words are inspired by God Himself.

These words, Jeremiah 29:11-13, offer solace and a promise for one's future: "'For I know the plans I have for you,' declares the Lord, 'plans to prosper you and not to harm you, plans to give you a hope and a future. Then you will call upon me and pray to me and I will listen to you. You will seek me and find me when you seek me with all your heart.'"

It's comforting to know that God is with us. He's never against us, but sometimes we turn our backs on God.

I trust in the Lord that He will provide for all my needs.

I believe my dreams will come true. These are the desires of my heart, and the Lord says in the Holy Bible that He will make all our desires of the heart come true, as God placed those desires into our hearts.

Someday I will have a house, be married and perhaps have children—"the American Dream!"

I want to raise my children, if I have any, as if doing so is the greatest job on Earth. I believe that parenting should come before all things, with the exception of the Lord.

On a cautionary note, my parents divorced when I was 10 years old, and a big factor—I have learned from both parents years later—was discipline. My parents couldn't agree on how to discipline me and my brother.

I would strongly encourage two people who plan to marry, or even before then, to sit down and discuss discipline: what it means to each party and how they both feel they should treat their children when they misbehave.

Speaking about love being faith and faith love, Galations 5:5-6 reads: "But by faith we eagerly await through the Spirit the righteousness for which we hope. The only things that count is faith expressing itself through love."

There is great promise in medicine today. Scientists are just now beginning to think that a gene causes schizophrenia. If they could "zap" the faulty gene, schizophrenia could be curable.

Great hope lies in AIDS and cancer research. President Clinton, in May of 1997, addressed a college graduation crowd and called on the need for the cure for AIDS; he committed himself to finding a cure for AIDS within the next decade and said that this promise parallels that of John F. Kennedy's to put a man on the moon before the year 1970.

Just as God is working through scientists working on finding cures, so does God work through each of us. This is explained perfectly in Romans 8:18-21: "And we know that in all things God works for the good of those who love him, who have been called according to his purpose."

I pray every day that everyone in this world will find love and have a better tomorrow than they had today! We all can become healthier, less prejudiced and more loving each day.

I pray for a cure for AIDS and cancer in the near future, so that no more people have to suffer needlessly.

Ever since I began high school, I've wanted to be a writer and a publicist when I grew up. Now that I'm writing as a volunteer part-time gives me great hope that one day I will be experienced enough to work for an entertainer as a publicist or assistant publicist.

In every article I have ever written, I have always tried to bring out some good in people in my writing. I always emphasize the positive, the upright, the inspirational. I'd be a great publicist!

Speaking on God's plans for each of us, Christ writes through John in 15:7-8: "If you remain in me and my words remain in you, ask whatever you wish, and it will be given to you. This is to my Father's glory, that you bear much fruit, showing yourselves to be my disciples."

When we decide to walk through life to eternity with Christ next to us, He puts an armor of protection around us. This is described in Romans 8:31: "What, then, shall we say in response to this? If God is for us, who can be against us?"

I loved going to Oxford, England, riding trains in Switzerland and northern, hilly Italy and taking in Michelangelo's sights in Florence.

I love to travel! You can go anywhere through books, but nothing beats being right there in person! I'm an adventurous traveler; there are very few places that I wouldn't want to see!

I've been to almost every state in the country. My favorite memories are of seeing the enormity of the Grand Canyon, the breath-taking rock formations out West and Mackinac Island in Michigan.

Mom and I rode mules down into the Grand Canyon. Was that exciting! The tour guide kept stopping so that my mule was at the corner where the trail curved; his hoofs kept slipping backwards and I thought, "God, please don't take me now. I want to live! Life is good!" Luckily, the mule and I emerged in one piece and not hurt seriously, thank God!

That night, mom, Dennis and I ate at the Grand Canyon Lodge. It was my 15th birthday, and while I was in the bathroom my parents ordered a birthday cake for me. 45 minutes later and all of us finished with our dinners, we waited. We saw the beautiful sunset. I asked, "What are we waiting for?" There wasn't much my Mom and Dennis could do; they said that they just wanted to take in the beautiful sights of the Grand Canyon. Soon thereafter, a parade of waiters and waitresses came out and presented me—to my great surprise!—a wonderfully-decorated cake. I was so thankful! What fun we had!

It took so long to bake the cake, our waitress explained, because of the high altitude we were at!

The rock formations out West are incredible! I was in awe just looking at them!

Mackinac Island was fun; we rode bikes around the island! It's quite popular among tourists to bike around the island, which is roughly a few miles in circumference.

I have great hope that one day I will be able to return to those beautiful sights! I encourage all of my readers to travel to these wonderful vacation spots. God is good, and all His creations, like His children, are made in his perfect image. If your desire is great enough to visit one of these vacation spots, God will provide a way if you seek Him and His perfect will for your life.

20

Scriptures

What is Gods' will for each of our lives? How do we know if we're walking in God's will or trying to do things our own way?

Prayer will lead you to God's will. So will these Scriptures I'd like to share with you to lift you up and keep you on the right track.

God wants us to be happy, and He will always be at our side whether we're in good or low spirits. This is clear in Psalm 121:1: "I will lift up mine eyes unto the hills, from when cometh my help."

Too often we put limits on our lives. As long as we aren't doing any harm to ourselves or others, we are on the right track. We don't believe we can make it, but the Lord says in Matthew 17:20: "Nothing shall be impossible unto you."

Worry will drag anyone down. We need to rid ourselves of any and all worry, knowing that the Lord is always with us. Psalm 55:22 says: "Cast thy burden upon the Lord, and He shall sustain thee."

Just as we banish worry from our lives, so must we also turn our backs on fear. We must affirm ourselves. Psalm 34:4 reads: "I sought the

Lord, and He heard me, and delivered me from all my fears." That's a powerful Scripture!

When we solve our problems —- learn from them—we need to keep in mind what the Lord said through John in 16:33: "In the world ye shall have tribulation; but be of good cheer; I have overcome the world." To live according to God's will for our lives, we must think deeply, clear our minds and use silence to creatively find ways to solve our problems.

Now that we are on the right track towards living out God's will for our lives, I'd like to share with you the benefits of abiding in God's will.

First off, once we turn to God He offers us protection. This is clear in Psalms 91:9-12: "If you make the Most High your dwelling —- even the Lord, who is my refuge—then no harm will befall you, no disaster will come near your tent. For He will command His angels concerning you to guard you in all your ways; they will lift you up in their hands, so that you will not strike your foot against a stone."

Next, God makes us productive members of society. John 15:5-8 reads: "I am the vine; you are the branches. If a man remains in me and I in him, he will bear much fruit; apart from me you can do nothing. If anyone does not remain in me, he is like a branch that is thrown away and withers; such branches are picked up, thrown into the fire and burned."

Finally, when we walk with Christ, He makes a provision for our lives. This is evident in John 15:7-8: "If you remain in me and my words remain in you, ask whatever you wish, and it will be given to you. This is to my Father's glory, that you bear much fruit, showing yourselves to be my disciples."

21

"Walk the Walk"

''Walk the Walk,'' held in the nation's capitol May 2, 1998, will live on in my heart and mind as an historical event with far-reaching and life-enhancing progress for lives touched by mental illness.

The annual event drew thousands and thousands of consumers and advocates. We all joined together to unite as a powerful voice for lives touched by mental illness.

Registration began at 9:30 a.m. After 45 minutes of speakers, who began at 10:00 a.m., the walk began from Freedom Square and headed one block towards the Capitol. The march then went around two more long blocks before finishing in Freedom Square.

Additional speakers lent their support for the care and rights of persons who have mental illness with their speeches which lasted another half hour after the walk, until about 11:40 a.m.

My brother met me at Ronald Reagan International Airport on the eve of Thursday, April 30. As we made our way to our hotel, via taxi, we saw the Capitol and memorials all lit up. What sights to see! John stayed with me the entire weekend and "Walked the Walk" with me!!!

Washington, D.C. is a clean, beautiful city! D.C. has numerous parks, and is green with life and blossoming cherry trees everywhere in Spring.

On Friday, John and I took in the Archives Museum and saw the Declaration of Independence and the Bill of Rights. We also visited the Aeronautical and Space Museum and the Art Museum. There were no tickets left for the day to get into the Holocaust Museum, so we didn't do that, but we did visit Holocaust Survivor Danny's House.

This stroll though the parks remains one of my top five favorite things we experienced in our four days in the nation's capitol.

After "Walk the Walk" on Saturday, John and I headed over to the nation's Capitol. We sat in the Senate and the House of Representatives' chambers, which are located at opposite ends of the Capitol building.

In the House, we saw the door that the President walks through and sat where the First Lady sits for the annual President's State of the Union address.

Saturday night, our last night in D.C., we took a night tour bus ride around Washington, D.C. We stopped at the Roosevelt Memorial, the Lincoln Memorial, the Washington Memorial and the Jefferson Memorial. We took in the Vietnam and Korean War Memorial, the outside of the White House and the Capitol.

John and I wanted to go inside the White House, but were told to get in line for tickets at 6:30 a.m. Then, with tickets, we'd have to wait until 2:30 p.m. to get in. Because we did so much sightseeing and walking, we decided that we would only visit the White House from the outside. I took a beautiful picture of the White House's front lawn.

Sunday morning, before checking out of our hotel, John and I took a couple of last-minute stops at the city's aquarium and Ford Theater where Lincoln was shot.

Besides the inside of the White House, the only sights I think we missed were the inside of the Supreme Court (we did walk past this) and the Smithsonian Museum (which we also walked past). There was so much we wanted to take in, so we didn't have enough time to go through both buildings like we would have wanted to.

"Walk the Walk" epitomizes the hope that we as a nation and as united persons with mental illness and advocates for the mentally ill will see within our lifetimes better treatments and care for persons with mental illness and their loved ones.

Participating in this event has made me, as a mentally ill person, stronger and prouder of who I am as a mentally ill person.

22

Condo

In 1999, I closed on a two-bedroom, two-bath condominium a few miles from my mom and Dennis' home. This is a dream come true for me and my family.

Buying a new home brings about feelings of exhilaration and anticipation!

Prior to the closing and after making an offer on the condo, I began to have buyer's remorse. I wondered whether or not I wanted to plunge into homeownership and take on more responsibilities.

After my closing, I began to question whether or not I made a sound decision in buying a new home for myself. Everyone told me it's normal to have these feelings.

I have two mortgage payments to make every month, in addition to recreation, maintenance and association fees.

I made a first offer on a more expensive condo and was turned down by the owner, who held out for more money for his condo.

The second condo I made an offer on—and was accepted—was the condo I really wanted anyway, as it has a most beautiful balcony.

Once I made an offer on the second condo, it took several days before receiving an acceptance. I could hardly wait to close on the second condo.

The condo I chose needed a great deal of work. Mom and Dennis helped tremendously by painting the entire condo. They also did many, many repairs to bring the condo to code for the closing.

I had new carpeting, tile and an air conditioning unit put in my condo. Dennis repaired a faulty water heater.

After everything was done, we had a big open house party! About 30 friends and family members came and brought me all sorts of kind gifts!

I enjoy the balcony at my condo. I like to sit out there and listen to beautiful birds. It's fun to sit on my balcony with a stereo headset on or simply read a good book out there. It's very peaceful and quiet where I live, and I relish these peaceful moments which help to clear my mind of a busy day's activities.

23

Conclusion/Late 20's "Present"

Lately I've been doing a lot of advocating for the mentally ill. I feel that it is God's will for my life right now to advocate for the mentally ill.

In December of 1999 President Clinton signed and passed an important legislation called the Ticket to Work/Work Incentive Improvement Act of 1999. This bill passed on the federal level with bipartisan support, paving the way for persons with mental illness to return to work part-time without losing their benefits.

Although this bill, called HR 1180, succeeded in becoming federal law, it must be passed on the state level to do any good for individuals who want to work but are limited by the present state laws.

The cores of the bill are as follow: The Ticket to Work section deals with work rehabilitation and training services; whereas, the Work Incentives Improvement Act addresses the Social Security Disability (SSDI) and Social Administration (SSA) policies which, once the state bill is passed, will allow beneficiaries to return to part-time work without losing one's benefits.

I was very active in writing letters and making many phone calls to important legislators on the federal and state levels.

Since August of 1997 I have worked as a writer. Since I cannot work for money and keep my benefits, I choose to volunteer my time and talents. I have written several news-feature articles.

Often I am the one to suggest story ideas, and sometimes my publisher/editor will ask me to write a piece on a certain person or place. The office I work in is rather small. Including the sales people, there are about 15 people who work there.

I work on Mondays, Wednesdays and Fridays. I am a good proof-reader and often my volunteer job doesn't have me come into the office unless there is editorial to proofread. I have written a few articles and conducted a couple of interviews over the phone from my home.

I attend a non-denominational church near my condo. We raise our hands to the Lord and some people are gifted in that they speak in tongues.

There is an aura in this church; you can just feel that God is there! I feel that everyone must come to the Lord sometimes in their life, and I believe this is necessary to go to heaven.

My family and friends, including my dad, are sources of support for me, as is my counselor who I see every week.

I recently completed a free TV production course which lasted 10 weeks. Its instructors taught all aspects of TV production: operating cameras and working in the control room. I'm excited! I'm trying to broaden my base as far as the kind of work I'd like to do and be trained in when I am able to work for money without losing my benefits!

My Dad is doing all right on chemotherapy, but I hope they put him on a new treatment which is supposed to be more effective in treating his cancer and has less side effects. This new treatment is still being tested.

My roommate is the same guy I lived with in the apartment for the mentally ill. Last night he and I went with a close friend to visit a good friend of ours who is at the local mental hospital I went to because she stopped taking her medications. It was a healing experience for me. You may recall that I thought people at a local mental hospital were trying to kill me while I was in that hospital in 1995. My friend was even in the same room that I was in.

It was healing for me to go to this local mental health hospital last night. I now have "re-thought" the situation and realize—just as when I thought my grandma was trying to kill me —- that it was my psychotic thinking on zero medications which produced these horrible feelings of doom. Now that it's five years later and I'm extremely stable on my medications I see things in another light. People aren't out to kill me or my family, I have learned through extensive therapy and helpful medications.

I'm trying to live a healthy life. It's not always easy, but it can be done. I have stopped watching all television; I get paranoid thoughts when I watch TV and, understandably, I feel more calm when I'm not watching TV.

My brother is making lots of money. He's not a Christian like I am. Sometimes I wonder why he's "making it" while I struggle month-to-month on my finances. I'm happy for my brother and everything he's accomplishing.

I have learned that it's best not to compare yourself to others. We each are here for different reasons. Maybe someday I will be rich. But, for now, I see clearly that God is using me to pave the way for better treatments of the mentally ill. It is a will that I gladly accept. This may take years; maybe breakthroughs in legislations and medications will come soon. Legislators and scientists around the country are working for these things.

I have hope that things will get better for our mentally ill. Some days it's scary to think about what God has for me, but having faith that He is using me now for better things helps me to keep an open perspective and a sense of security. I refuse to let mental illness interfere with my sense of happiness.

Lately I've been feeling obsessive about people in my life and my anxiety has been increasing. My psychiatrist recently put me on Anafranil to curb these symptoms. I've only been taking this medicine for a short period of time now but I already feel much better.

My roommate of three years told me recently that he's moving out to live with his mom and grandparents. They're not going to charge him any rent, so he will be able to save some money. I wish him well.

God will show me, one day at a time, what he wants me to do once all this important legislation is passed for the mentally ill.

There is a lot more that needs to be accomplished when it comes to helping the mentally ill. We need better legislations, a Bill of Patient's Rights and the security of knowing that our medications won't be compromised to horrific older medications which barely work. There are great medications out there today to help combat mental illness; let's keep these helpful, most beneficial drugs in our consumers' hands and let's lobby for even better medications to treat serious mental illness, such as my paranoid schizophrenia.

I'd like to work as a writer or assistant publicist for a show.

When it comes down to the end, it's people that matter the most. Life is about touching others' lives in a loving, sincere way. This alone supersedes material wealth.

Families and friends who are there for you—such as mine are—through the thick and thin are the people who one must treasure close to one's heart.

I have found that faith in God can carry you through the best and worst of times. God loves each of us so very much, and it breaks His heart to see us stray away from Him. But through it all, God is faithful. Trust in the Lord and He will never leave you. God Bless!

About the Author

A 1993 university graduate with a Bachelor's degree in English, Chip Correll also graduated with top honors from a local community college.

An avid traveler, Chip frequently flies to visit with his father, step-mother and brother.

Chip enjoys going to the movies and is currently co-writing with a friend a screenplay about the lives of three college students.

Chip is a political activist who has done a great deal for the betterment of human services for the mentally ill.

A loyal Christian, Chip tries to keep a perspective in his busy life. God comes first, then family and then work. He reads the Holy Bible often.

Chip is an active member of the National Alliance for the Mentally Ill (NAMI).

www.ingramcontent.com/pod-product-compliance
Lightning Source LLC
Chambersburg PA
CBHW031240280526
45784CB00004B/1658